CRITICAL

DRIFT

CAROLINE BERGVALL

NIGHTBOAT BOOKS BROOKLYN & CALLICOON, NY

ISBN 978-1-937658-20-5

Design and typesetting by Pablo Lavalley
Text set in Vendetta and Simplon BP

Cover image by Tom Martin.
Macro treatment of aircraft sighting photograph,
in "Report on the "Left-To-Die Boat," 2012.

Cataloging-in-publication data is available
from the Library of Congress

Nightboat Books
Brooklyn & Callicoon, NY
www.nightboat.org

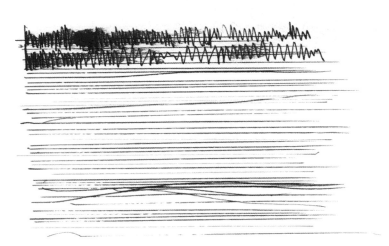

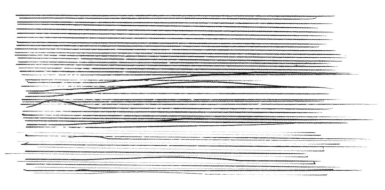

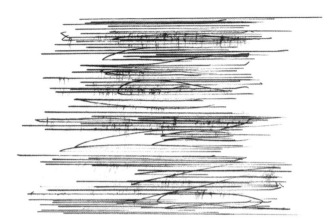

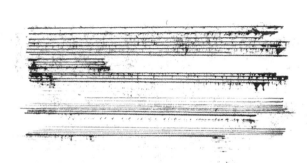

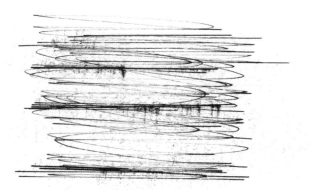

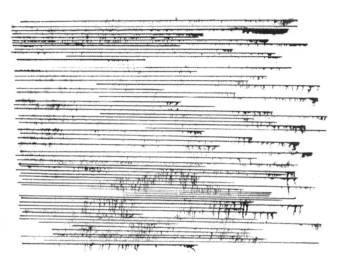

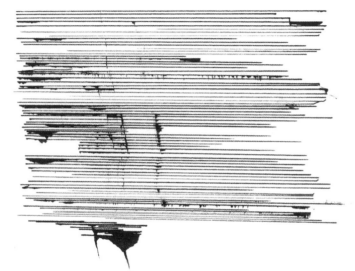

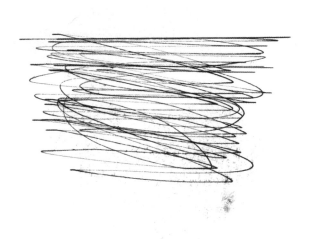

SEAFARER

Let me speak my true journeys own true songs

I can make my sorry tale right soggy truth

sothgied sodsgate some serious wrecan my ship

sailing rekkies tell Hu ic how ache wracked from

travel gedayswindled oft thrownabout bitterly

tested gebanging head keeling at every beating

waves What cursed fool grimly beshipped

couldnt get signs during many a nightwacko

caught between whats gone ok whats coming

on crossing too close to the cliffs Blow wind

blow, anon am I

Cold gesprung weary worn were my feet frost
bound in the ice-blinding clamour of kulla
city sank further seafaring is seafodder heart
humbling Could scarcely move or draw my
breath cursed with nightmares gewacked by
seachops gave up all parts of me on gebattered
ship Yet a hungor innan mind stole me to more
weird comas let me let me let me let me freeze
Blow wind blow, anon am I

Stormed by winter land fell away This one
doesnt know fact noman knows that one has
no weight sea folded enfolded me ok loved ones
ok landed fullness ok field promises Cant ache
for hem nor hem for ache nor praises nor raised
loveskirts nor rings nor harping nor allround
loveliness How ache miserable now heaven
knows last living soul behung with ice castles
Hail hagl hard nothing else geheard gehurt but
sky butting against sea against sky against sea
gainst seagainsky Blow wind blow, anon am I

Sailed on due north nord norÞ norð norit norÞe norh northt give or
take a few transmission errors when steering by the sun ok the stars
ok prevailing winds ok birds ok feeding grounds Due north skirting
shorelines rock ledging from view to view following tidal streams
visibility good horizon divided navigation possible Safe northing
for three days for fifteen days for seven days for thirty days for forty
days biforen hitting the banks ok knolls of the north-sea holes
Here nocturnal shoals herrings silvertrail release a way the norþerne
sword avalon

When you fish for the herring they rule your life they swim at night youve got to be out there at night waiting for them to swim plus its a wonder too you see to pick one of these little fish up the nets vibrant with life rrrrr like that the numbers its only one of millions and millions and millions when the little people swim up proply it might be waiting 200 miles from aberdeen or the norwegian deepwater or off shields if the herring are there you have to go get them Come on spin up my darlings

Going north by needle and stone from ireland to orkney to shetland to faroe Going north for stockfisc from lynn to scotland to bergen to the lofot isles Going northlike casting lead off greenland thinking it be thule Shoring up in vinland taking it for greenland island-hopping To the island of sheep To the isle of joy To the land of women To the soporific well To the fiery mountain Circling round the crystal pillar Setting camplike on a hump Back down to the isle of madeira thinking it be faroe Laughing all the way to charing cross thinking it be bank

Going north like getting to china westward way crossing the
atlantic Left the shore turned sailor the rays worked round to the
nor'nor'east the west sea is the north sea east of iceland all men are
easterners a shipmate known as william brown gudrid gudridur
fared to greenland on to vinland mary lacy northing it as william
cavendish rachel young northing it as billy bridle elizabeth bowden
did her work well as a strong active boy on this ship mary bonney
anne read pirates fantabulosa Hear, hear all scarper to sea

Going north like going south Land upraises in saucershaped world
the world is flat when maps are round round when maps are flat
phanomt spectr vessels warp inout of timeholes abandon al loose
fittings ed warfloats cargo steamers gast g ost h h love skips lady
lovibond in the goodwin sands the baychimo gost ship of the
arctic the tuxedo royale festering in hartlepool with her revolving
dancefloor the octavius petrif off the north west passage captain
froz n at his desk still writing in his log At the end of space there
is no restaurant Wheres north from here from hér from her

Ottar said that Northmen land was very swyde long and very swyde
narrow told his ohman that he to the north of ealra northmen
northmost lived said that he lived on them land northward long tha
westsæ said that that land is swipe long north but hit is all waste
but for a few sticks with Finnas hunting on wintra and on sumera
fishing be there sea said that he would fan out hu longe that land
nortright lies and whether any one to the north of the westenne lived
then fared he northright see them lande

Ottar said then sailed he sunny southright by land swa swa he made
five days gesailing there lies there a great ea great river up in on that
land that high up in on tha ea that river fare them not cos them
land was all gelived on othre side there ea river no not met he none
living the land since he from his own home had fared and he had
all the way wasteland on tha starboard but for fisher and fugler and
hunters and that were just Finnas and he had always a wide sea on
tha beckboard

Ottar said all the way that weste land on tha starboard and that wide widsæ on tha beckboard for three days then was he swa far norther than whalehuntan ever go farap then fared he more northright swa farther swa he made them other three days sailing then that land there turned eastright, or the sea in that land nysse hwæðer didnt know which butan knew that he there bad westan winds and then northan then sailed tha east down land swa swa he made four days gesailing there should he there bidan rhythm northwind wait then that land begs there southright or the sea in that land nysse hwæðer he didnt know which

The fair wind failed. The wind dropped. Winds were unfavourable straightaway. The favourable wind dropped and they were beset by storms so that they made little progress. Then the wind dropped and they were beset by winds from the north and fog; for many days they did not know where they were sailing. The fair wind failed and they wholly lost their reckoning. They did not know from what direction. Driven here and there. The fog was so dense that they lost all sense of direction and lost their course at sea. There was much fog and the winds were light and unfavourable. They drifted far and wide on the high sea. Most of those on board completely lost their reckoning. The crew had no idea in which direction they were steering. A thick fog which did not lift for days. The ship was driven off course to land. They were tossed about at sea for a long time and failed to reach their destination. We embarked and sailed but a fog so thick covered us that we could scarcely see the poop or the prow of the boat

Then the wind ddroppe and they were beset by w inds from then
orth and fog for manyd ays they did not know where they were
sailing Thef air wind f ailed and they wholly l ost their reck their
reckoning did not not know from what direction D riven here and
there The f og was sodense that they l ost all ss ense of dirrrtion and
l ost thr course at sea There was much fog and the w inds were light
and unf and unfavourable They driftedf ar and wide on the high sea
Mo stof those onboard completly l ost l ost l ost their reckoning Th
ec rew had no idea in which direction they were ststeering A thick
fo g which d i d n ot l ift for days The sh ip was driven offf course tol
and They were ossted about astea for a longt ime and f iled tor each
their destination We mbarkt and sailed but a fog so th but a fog so
th but a fog so th th th thik k overed us that we could scarcely see
the poop or the prow of the boa t

str ght w   Th f r w nd f l d Th w nd dr pp d Th f v r bl

w nd dr pp d nd th   w r b s t b st rms s th t th   m d

l ttl pr gr ss Th n th w nd dr pp d nd th   w r b s t by w nds

fr m the n rth nd f g f r m ny d ys th y d d n t kn w wh re th y

w r s l ng Th f r w nd f l d nd th y wh ll l st th r r ck th r

r ck n ng Th y d d n t kn w fr m wh t d r ct n D r v n h r nd

th r Th f g w s s d ns th t th y l st ll ss ns f d rrrt n nd

l st thr c rs t s Th r w s m ch f g nd th w nds w r l ght

 nd unf nd nf v r bl They dr ft d f r nd w d   n th h gh s

M st f th se nb rd c mpl tly l st l st l st th r r ck n ng Th

 c r w h d

n d   n wh ch d r ct n th y w r st st ring   th ck f g wh ch d

d n t l ft f r d ys The sh p

w s dr ven ff f c rse t l nd Th y w r sst d b t st f r

l ng t me and f led t r ch th r

d st n tion W mb rkt nd s l d b t f g s th b t f g s th b t
 f g s th th th th th k k v r d

 s th t w c ld sc rc ly s th p p rth pr w f th b t f the
b t of the b t the b

b s t b st rms s th t th m d l ttl pr gr ss Th n th w nd
dr pp d nd th w r b s t by w

The sh p w s dr ven fff c rse t l nd Th y w r sst d b t
 st f r

l ngt me and f led t r ch th r d st n tion W mb rkt nd s l d
b t f g

s th b t f g s th b t f g s th th th th th k k v r d s th t w
c ld sc rc ly s th p p rth pr w f th b t t t t t t t t t t t t
t t t t t t t t t t t t t t t t t t t t t t t t t t t t t t t t t t t t t t t t t t t t t t t t t t t t t t

t t t t t t t t t t t t t t t t t t t t t t t t t t t t t t t t t t t t t t t t t t t t t t t t t t t t t

t t t t t t t t t t t t t t t t t t t t t t t t t t t t t t t t t t t t t t t t t t t t t t t t t t t t t

t t t t t t t t t t t t t t t t t t t t t t t t t t t t t t t t t t t t t t t t t t t t t t t t t t t t t

t t t t t t t t t t t t t t t t t t t t t t t t t t t t t t t t t t t t t t t t t t t t t t t t t t t t t

t t t t t t t t t t t t t t t t t t t t t t t t t t t t t t t t t t t t t t t t t t t t t t t t t t t t t

t t t t t t t t t t t t t t t t t t t t t t t t t t t t t t t t t t t t t t t t t t t t t t t t t t t t t

t t t t t t t t t t t t t t t t t t t t t t t t t t t t t t t t t t t t t t t t t t t t t t t t t t t t t

t t t t t t t t t t t t t t t t t t t t t t t t t t t t t t t t t t t t t t t t t t t t t t t t t t t t t

t t t t t t t t t t t t t t t t t t t t t t t t t t t t t t t t t t t t t t t t t t t t t t t t t t t t t

t t t t t t t t t t t t t t t t t t t t t t t t t t t t t t t t t t t t t t t t t t t t t t t t t t t t t

t t t t t t t t t t t t t t t t t t t t t t t t t t t t t t t t t t t t t t t t t t t t t t t t t t t t t

t t t t t t t t t t t t t t t t t t t t t t t t t t t t t t t t t t t t t t t t t t t t t t t t t t t t t

t t t t t t t t t t t t t t t t t t t t t t t t t t t t t t t t t t t t t t t t t t t t t t t t t t t t t

t t t t t t t t t t t t t t t t t t t t t t t t t t t t t t t t t t t t t t t t t t t t t t t t t t t t t

t t t t t t t t t t t t t t t t t t t t t t t t t t t t t t t t t t t t t t t t t t t t t t t t t t t t t

t t t t t t t t t t t t t t t t t t t t t t t t t t t t t t t t t t t t t t t t t t t t t t t t t t t t t

t t t t t t t t t t t t t t t t t t t t t t t t t t t t t t t t t t t t t t t t t t t t t t t t t t t t t

t t t t t t t t t t t t t t t t t t t t t t t t t t t t t t t t t t t t t t t t t t t t t t t t t t t t t

t t t t t t t t t t t t t t t t t t t t t t t t t t t t t t t t t t t t t t t t t t t t t t t t t t t t t

t t t t t t t t t t t t t t t t t t t t t t t t t t t t t t t t t t t t t t t t t t t t t t t t t t t t t t

t t t t t t t t t t t t t t t t t t t t t t t t t t t t t t t t t t t t t t t t t t t t t t t t t t t t t t

t t t t t t t t t t t t t t t t t t t t t t t t t t t t t t t t t t t t t t t t t t t t t t t t t t t t t t

t t t t t t t t t t t t t t t t t t t t t t t t t t t t t t t t t t t t t t t t t t t t t t t t t t t t t t

t t t t t t t t t t t t t t t t t t t t t t t t t t t r t t t t t t t t t t t t t t t t t t t t L t t t t t

t t t t t t t t t t t t t t t t t t t t t t t t t t t t t t t t t t t t t t t t t t t t t t t t t t t t t t

t t t t t t t t t t t t t t t t t t t t t t t t t t t t t t t t t t t t t t t t t t t t t t t t t t t t t t

t t t t t t t t t t t t t t t t t t t t t t t t t t t t t t t t t t t t t t t t t t t t t t t t t t t t t t

t t t t t t t t t t t t t t t t t t t t t t t t t t t t t t t t t t t t t t t t t t t t t t t t t t t t t t

t t t t t t t t t t t t t t t t t t t t t t t t t t t t t t t t t t t t t t t t t t t t t t t t t t t t t t

t t t t t t t t t t t t t t t t t t t t t t t t t t t t t t t t t t t t t t t t t t t t t t t t t t t t t t

t t t t t t t t t t t t t t t t t t t t t t t t t t t t t t t t t t t t t t t t t t t t t t t t t t t t t t

t t t t t t t t t t t t t t t t t t t t t t t t t t t t t t t t t t t t t t t t t t t t t t t t t t t t t t

t t t t t t t t t t t t t t t t t t t t t t t t t t t t t t t t t t t t t t t t t t t t t t t t t t t t t t

t t t t t t t t t t t t t t t t t t t t t t t t t t t t t t t t t t t t t t t t t t t t t t t t t t t t t t

t t t t t t t t t t t t t t t t t t t t t t t t t t t t t t t t t t t t t t t t t t t t t t t t t t t t t t

t t t t t t t t t t t t t t t t t t t t t t t t t t t t t t t t t t t t t t t t t t t t t t t t t t t t t t

t t t t t t t t t t t t t t t t t t t t t t t t t t t t t t t t t t t t t t t t t t t t t t t t t t t t t t

t t t t t t t t t t t t t t t t t t t t t t t t t t t t t t t t t t t t t t t t t t t t t t t t t t t t t t t t t t t
t t t t t t t t t t t t t t t t t t t t t t t t t t t t t t t t t t t t t t t t t t t t t t t t t t t t t t t t t t t
t t t t t t t t t t t t t t t t t t t t t t t t t t t t t t t t t t t t t t t t t t t t t t t t t t t t t t t t t t t
t t t t t t t t t t t t t t t t t t t t t t t t t t t t t t t t t t t t t t t t t t t t t t t t t t t t t t t t t t t
t t t t t t t t t t t t t t t t t t t t t t t t t t t t t t t t t t t t t t t t t t t t t t t t t t t t t t t t t t t
t t t t t t t t t t t t t t t t t t t t t t t t t t t t t t t t t t t t t t t t t t t t t t t t t t t t t t t t t t t
t t t t t t t t t t t t t t t t t t t t t t t t t t t t t t t t t t t t t t t t t t t t t t t t t t t t t t t t t t t
t t t t t t t t t t t t t t t t t t t t t t t t t t t t t t t t t t t t t t t t t t t t t t t t t t t t t t t t t t t
t t t t t t t t t t t t t t t t t t t t t t t t t t t t t t t t t t t t t t t t t t t t t t t t t t t t t t t t t t t
t t t t t t

t go

t go off

t go off course

t go off course hafville

t be lost forvillet hafville Ache come off course hafville

Did not go where I was knowing hafville Had fear wildering hafville

For a minute there I lost myself Totally at sea lost myway tossed misted

lost mywill in the fog hafville hafville my love

Major Tom hafville

Li Bai hafville

Rimbaud hafville

Shelley hafville

Amelia Earhart hafville

Jeff Buckley hafville

Spalding Gray hafville

Virginia Woolf hafville

Albert Ayler hafville

Reinaldo Arenas hafville

Hart Crane hafville

Ingeborg Bachmann hafville

When you rise from the dead,
when I rise from the dead,
the hangman will hang at the gate
the hammer will sink into the sea

Kom ut av kursen hafville Secgan at come hafvillur ok darkens
ok myrkr ok hafvillur ok þokur ok hafvillur Cannot pokker see
through this þokur Hwær hwanon never knew hu how to steer
out of this rook this moss droomly wetter stoutair mattersea thick
dank shadoway Lost lost all reckoning the sea coagulated All wats
not-light all wats not-dark Déadlockit Beat bells! Blow foghorns!
Storm the ceiling! Set my head on fire! Lightup! this d arkness for a
bearing thour pis halla

Beat bells blow foghorns! Gebangbang for rumbly lowe!

When will the wind come? Where will the wind from come?

Will it come from the naught, bringing phobias and rationing?

Will it come from the soot, bringing droughts and epidemics?

Will it come from the feast, fleeding crops and arteries?

Will it come from the waste, bringing seizures and military uprisings?

When will the wind come? Where will the wind from come?

Will it come from the clog, causing jellyfish fission shutdown?

Will it come from the leak, bringing mass dispersion radiation?

When will the wind come? Where will the wind from come?

Will it be an empty confusing windup? Will it be a tempestuous hooley?

Will it be a blippy huff 'n puff? Will it be a good proper piner?

Heigh Ho and up she rises! Heigh Ho and up she goes!

Beat bells! Blow foghorns! Loud metal gebangbang for rumbly love!

Dearly wonky woruld Hung albatross Oceans
glued infloating tarwings willing swan-song
Goose me up! Give me outlines! Laughing
gannets mullymacs fulmars curlews godwits
Show me the wave! Powerful arctic birds inout
of the rollers cranes goldeneagles shearwaters
pole to pole longhaul navigators Show me the
wave! Whaup gulls yap yap yap yap firebirds
griffins dingbats newly released transgenic flying
organisms prescient caladrius what warns of ills
terns stearns oncwæð what storm the fishing
beats Show me! Fly me! Ships with their crews
in the sky ships with their crews were plainly
seen in the sky this year fishing for cloud nine
mægahelium Here from hurry me free forms
Blow wind blow, anon am I

Thats why he ah wat gets lifes winnings lined
with measures unbeaten by the city flunks out
of windcraze fewles of muck offscoffs forbidding
oceanpaths Keeps a safe percentage ice melts in
deer bay raising speculations about the increased
trades benefits of the north east passage Keeps
a safe percentage merchant vessels cross the
icefree north coasts between europe and asia
its a shortcut on a planetary scale this narrow
passage between a sinking rock and a rising
whirlpool Cant wait for total meltdown Keeps a
safe percentage Blow wind blow, anon am I

Thats why he ah wat gets happily gedrunk
laughs off dark nihtscua nightsky nightclouds
shadowy northan snows earthless orphans
hurdled in containers noodled on plastic beach
in the corner coldest of the storm Days now
clasping at my cracking scin noman to steer
the failing structure Im a hostage of the waves
floating in my coffin I have lost all my papers all
I had with me Oneman gone thats all theyll say
Oneman gone, thats all theyll say Blow wind
blow, anon am I

Thats why crossing high streams on gebattered
ships mind moves nomad with all tha t-tossing
Thats why never one so proud and bold what
goes seafaring without mægaworry ohman of
being broken into code Ferð to feran far to fare
Ferð to feran feor to go further heonan further
hereon go forth Farout to the four winds to the
outlands Trip it journey wayfaring outvoyage to
geseek others plucked from this eard this earp
this harp ok the bearded geese Blow wind blow,
anon am I

To the northan ne north To the eastan ne east
To the westan ne west nor to the southan Nor is
gemynd my mind Nor hjarta in my heart Nor the
bane of my bones Nor the lime in my limbs Nor
does a beacon guide my back Nor is she aboard
ship Nor does ever anything wats unknowingly
known or knowingly unknowned abakward or
frontweird befree up a way for certain Thats why
ache a have da long one must find the horizon
hump ache a have da longing must follow the
wave Blow wind blow, anon am I

When there was blossoming when boroughs
take with blossom Sumer is icumen in Lhude
sing cuccu! Birdpods grow on the barnacle
tree What gorgeous mingling ok lovesongs ok
honeysuckling ok allround horniness Hear,
hear heaving with tidal thoughts hustled from
all tha t-turning the mind aroused gewakes the
sleepwrecked lingers in the wide scarpers to sea
Blow wind blow, anon am I

Rushed my skip to sky Sailed straight into the
hammer green thunnor wall electromagnetic
warptides wavelengths mindgawping nocturnal
flare ups rise from deep There are dark stars
There are arctic attacks See the lights! Sing the
merry dancers in all the hollows of the weruld
There whistling crackling brattle harp-welling
infolds spirit call at the poles magnetic heart
Blow wind blow, anon am I

Due naught amidst my old-ones fishermen
whaling girls what filled the decks with haerinc
stockfisc baggit halibut dab haddock plaice
flounder mackrel in abundance Kom on spin
up my skraelings hauled up shrimpis squides
globsters blobs meeremaides delfyns rorquals
Fought off the kraken the belching hafgufa the
heather-backed whale almighty fastitocalon
all long gone to high blue Belly up each and
everyone dead silver glory Blow wind blow,
anon am I

Sailed on to red tides of nonpoint source
to the sea of mercury island-hopping To the
abyssal plains To isles of dumping To knolls
of wild plastic To rigs of leaking To the flaming
scrap swamps circled round pillars of solid
scitta upsetting camp on a heap thinking it be
homelike Shoring up alongside floats of glued
birdwings ok exploding whales that are family
that are war stars that are ghost gongs that are
bone sounds that are ropes that bear the load
of days that are nihts thár are shorelines that
are human shiploads hostage of the outbounds
abandoned skiffs that are anchors on the mind
ok squatter settlements Blow wind blow,
anon am I

What one doesnt know fact nofool knows
that nowind filled my sails gold holds nogold
breath nobreath Troubled treks kneel on land
What is land heaven knows spirits rap from the
super highwhale to the vastest knot There are
abandoned vessels ok heart sightings ok lifted
anchors ok sky showers ok allround vanysshynge
Thats why Thats why Dream Bro Sis asleep in the
sand Of all that lives ece stondad nothing stands
but deeds ok songs and songs that dream deeds
that awake the mind Lastwords enwrap the work
of living with the ocean washing over Blow wind
blow, anon am I

There comes a great wave upward through
the spine Lifts the weather from its sorrow
Releases wingspan love precipitation Releases
the hanging figure from its hanging Lifted I load
my vessel with praise cargo oceanic it is Thankful
Thankful Thankful juices nerve-fluid heat up
quickly crawl Up the sword to the waking crown
softens salt-stiffened limb rises Up thru the feet
Up thru the legs thankful Up thru the pelvis Up
thru the solar plexus thankful Up thru the heart
Up thru the throat thankful Up thru the head
Up thru the silvered slivered truth Up thru the
unfolding wetter Uprises her great wave Oceanic
it is Blow wind blow, anon am I

No mooring no dragged anchorage not ever no
more no mere keeping it togeÞer the lines are
rigged my heart unfools walks the waters plows
the wisdom of the wilds Travelling large Days are
gewitnessed recall that sails were made for filling
that love was made for blessing Blow wind blow,
anon am I

Sealike sky falls into skylike ocean scatter skylike
shudder sealike A ship comes at me in all her
folds Each adoubt undoubted Each adriven by
the roll of coursing light packed ice melts with
each passing monad I will dwell in her sails I
will die as a wave among shearwaters ok petrels
enduring longhaul migrants Come cover your
span around me Should I capsize floodways Let
the whales have me todaeg Let me fold into the
fattened tissue of these large gentle ocean giants
Eagles die Kinsmen die You yourself will die One
thing never dies the fate of the honoured dead
Happy heilir are they who win for themselves
kindly words • In ealle tid • Oman •

Blow wind blow, anon am I

Everything passes into everything

Anon I pass to everything

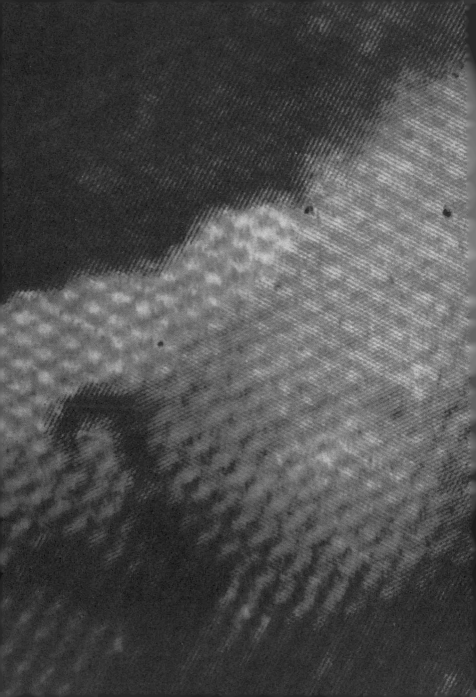

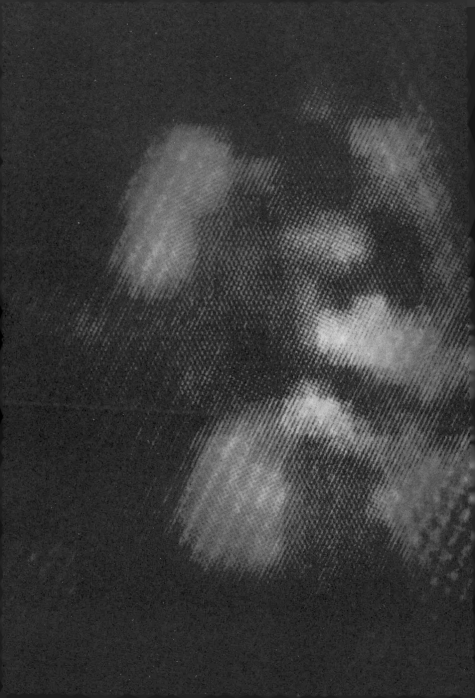

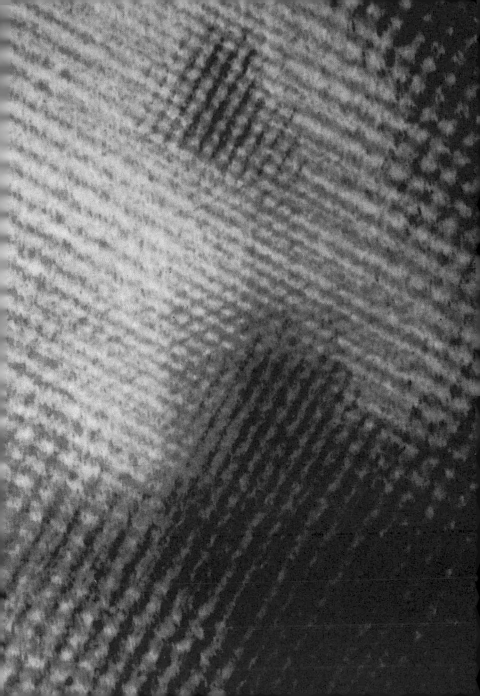

REPORT

On March 27, 2011 a ~10 m rubber boat overloaded with 72 migrants departed the port of Gargash adjacent to the Medina of Tripoli, Libya. This vessel was bound for Lampedusa Island, Italy 160 nm (nautical miles) to the north northwest.

The boat was provided by the Libyan army.

The boat was a rubber ship, a zodiac type plastic vessel, 10 meter long and with a capacity to carry max 25 people.

On the vessel there were 72 people including three children. 60 had been gathered in the nearby camp. A group of 12 people were brought to the point of departure just before leaving port.

There were seven people from Nigeria, six from Ghana, five from Sudan and seven from Eritrea, all of the 47 others were from Ethiopia.

At the moment of departure they contested being forced to travel in such a vessel.

With little choice, they embarked.

The survivors' testimonies differ on the date of departure.

Working backwards starting from the moment when the distress call was placed, we can establish the time and date of departure as between 2-3am Libyan time, or 00:00-01:00 GMT, on 27 March 2011.

The migrants were given a GPS, a compass and a Thuraya satellite phone. No food or water was provided.

The vessel was equipped with a Yamaha motor of 37 horsepower. Twelve tanks with a capacity of 20 litres of petrol each were provided. The migrants were told that this amount of fuel should allow them to reach Lampedusa and that the trip should have lasted around 18 hours.

The boat seems to have moved at a speed of less than 5 knots covering 66.6 nautical miles in around 15 hours.

At 14:55 GMT Rome MRCC received a notice from a French aircraft describing a small rubber boat with approx. 50 people on-board. It located the position of the migrants vessel as follows: LAT 33°40' N, LONG 13°05' E.

The migrants noticed an aircraft flying high above them.

The aircraft was white and not a helicopter but rather a small patrolling aircraft.

Rome MRCC provided a photograph of the rubber boat taken from the aircraft itself.

After approximately 15-18 hours at sea they called Father Zerai because they were about to run out of fuel.

At the time we called Father Mussie we had not even covered half the distance.

There were several calls exchanged because the driver was not able to read the boat's GPS instrument and could not provide the exact GPS coordinates of the boat.

The connection between Father Mussie and the migrants was made difficult due to failing batteries on the GPS.

Rome MRCC confirmed that they logged Father Zeria's call on 27 March at 16.28 GMT.

Thuraya, the satellite phone company, was contacted by Rome MRCC at 16:40GMT. It provided the location of the satellite device at 16:52 at LAT 33°58'.2 N, LONG 012°55'.8 E. approximately half the distance between Tripoli and Lampedusa.

Rome MRCC sent several distress signals, the first an Enhanced group Call (EGC) broadcast to all ships transiting in the Sicily Channel at 18:54 GMT via the Immarsat C system.

It also informed specific parties such as Malta and Nato headquarters allied command in Naples.

Priority code DISTRESS. Boat with about 68 passengers, probably in difficulty. All ships transiting in the area are requested to keep a sharp lookout and reporting any sighting urgently at MRCC Rome.

Due to the recent embargo on Libya, this particular area under NATO catchment was teeming with ships. We can estimate that at least 38 naval assets had been in operation in the waters off the coast of Libya for at least some time between 27 March and 10 April.

Twelve nations provided naval assets to enforce the embargo.

Using a synthesis of Automatic Ship Identification systems as well as surveillance and intelligence means, NATO verified shipping activity in the region to separate legitimate commercial, humanitarian and private traffic from suspicious vessels that warranted closer inspection.

Both on 28 and 29 March a large number of ships were in the area, some at distance of between 20 and 30 nautical miles to the migrants boat. Although we are not currently able to identify whether they were military or commercial or their nationality.

Ships transiting through the embargo area were required to notify NATO of their cargo and destination.

The maritime space was also closely monitored by several aircrafts.

More than 350 aircraft are involved in some capacity either enforcing the no-fly zone or protecting the civilian populace.

NATO/coalition naval and aerial assets were equipped with technologies that offered an extremely high sensing capacity geared both towards combat operations and to the monitoring of the Maritime Surveillance Area.

What we do is link up all our radar images together, all the ships. We are also working with aircrafts that are tracking vessels. And from that we have a full picture of all vessels in the area.

After a few hours a helicopter arrived.

Witnesses state it bore the English writing ARMY or RESCUE ARMY.

It circled around 4-5 times and came closer. It came very close to us down, we showed them our babies, we showed them we finished oil, we tell them please help us.

I think I saw them take pictures. I think I saw a photo camera or something like that.

This description is consistent with protocols for vessel identifications missions.

The helicopter left without providing assistance.

The migrants believed they would be soon rescued.

This is the rescue! we are safe.

The captain then threw the GPS, satellite phone and compass into the water because he was afraid that if the SAR team found these on board he would be identified as a smuggler and be deported.

Thuraya identified the last signal from the migrants satellite phone at 19.08 GMT with the position 34 07.11 N' – 12 53.24' E, 9 nautical

miles further in the direction of Lampedusa.

Waiting for rescue the migrants remained in place for 4-5 hours. By then, it was the middle of the night.

The migrants decided to start moving again despite the little fuel and with no communication means and with a small plastic compass attached to a belt. This compass and the stars were their only means of orientation at this point.

Once they resumed movement the migrants tried to approach some fishermen around them to ask for help.

When the fishermen saw the migrants arriving, they drew in their nets and sailed away swiftly.

During this time the migrants navigated for short stretches in random directions, without following the direction of Lampedusa but moving from one boat to the other.

This encounter with the fishermen was immediately followed by the re-appearance of what appeared to be the same helicopter. This time the military on-board lowered eight bottles of water and small packets of biscuits, both of which had Italian writing on them, and

left again.

The migrants encountered one more Tunisian fishing boat which gave them direction to Lampedusa in Arabic. The fisherman pointed in the direction and said:

four hours

The migrants vessel started to navigate again with the outboard engine for approx. four hours or eight to nine hours.

They were moving at greatest possible speed and consumed all the remaining 20 litres of fuel.

The vessel kept sailing until the following morning, until there was daylight again.

The sun rose at around 7:00 GMT on 28 March.

We have concluded that the motor ran out of fuel and the vessel began to drift between 6.00 GMT and 8.00 GMT on 28 March 2011.

Two time/position possibilities for the start of the drift:

The vessel started to drift at 06:00GMT (after 5 hours navigation) 22.2 nm NNW of last GPS position.

The vessel started to drift at 08:00 GMT (after 7 hours navigation) 31.1 nm NNW of last GPS position.

From the morning of the 28 March 2011, the migrants found themselves drifting in high waves for which their small, overcrowded rubber boat was unfit.

The sea was very dark with too much waves and wind. We lost our direction. From then on and for several days we dont know anything.

Left without food or water, the migrants began drinking sea-water as well as their own urine mixed with toothpaste.

After 2-3 days of this weather people started to die. The number of people increased daily. First two, then four, then five or six people died everyday.

While drifting the migrants sighted the lights of boats in the distance during the night.

During the night we would see the lights of other big boats in the distance,

we could not see them but the reflection of their lights looked like a city in the distance.

After 5-6 days of drifting in bad weather the migrants' vessel encountered a military ship.

They circled around us, three times, until they came very close, 10 meters. We are watching them, they are watching us. We are showing them the dead bodies. We drank water from the sea to show them we were thirsty. The people on the boat took pictures, nothing else.

This encounter occurred 5-6 days after the beginning of the drift in the storm.

It is most likely that the encounter with the military ship occurred between the 3rd and 4th April.

The military vessel left without providing them with any assistance.

We knew that we would die little-by-little.

For the last four days of drifting they could see the Libyan coast.

We could see buildings at night. The driver thought it was Malta but Nigerians on the boat said no these are the hotels built by Gaddafi in Tripoli.

During the last days of drifting almost all migrants seem to have lost consciousness or were in a very bad physical state.

The wind and the sea made us drift on Libyan land, to a small village near Misrata. When we reached that place we didn't know it was Libya, we thought it was Italy! When we reached the land one girl died within the hour.

The military took the ten of us to a pharmacy. They only gave us a bit of water and took us to prison in Zlitan. We spent three days there. Without food. One more of our brothers died there because of lack of food.

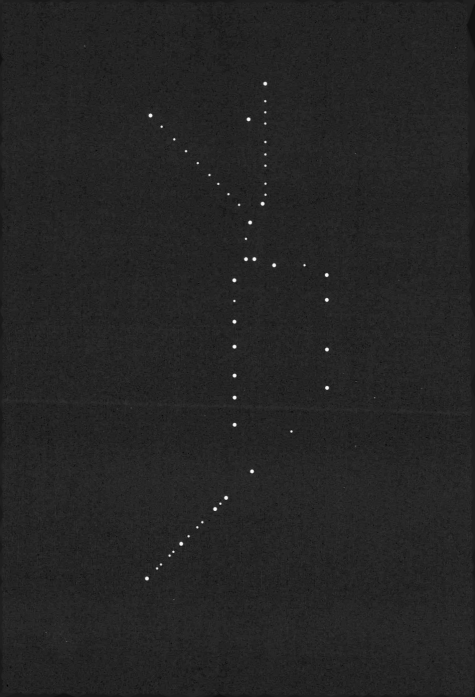

SHAKE

Gattir allar gates guess us all

adur gangi fram

others go forward

um skodast skyli

um skyggnast skyli

em shadows em shudder

Því at ovist er at vita

unknowing is to know

hvar ovinir each unknowing

sitja a fleti fyrir

sits by fleeting fires fireflies

Guests are in come
where shall so sit
soft are sisters
so a burning skull
go sing em freest first

Elders are berries
ok solar syn ok solar sight
ok seeing matter hopes
better alive than unalive
not lost at life
with lust for life ok ok

The room was busy
the living were noisy
crowding out the place
the dead were marching through
noone was paying attention
thats when I started to

I started to shake
ok ok when I started to
scook push sharken churn
ok wander ok scacan
thats when I started to shake

When the shaking starts
let the shaking
when the shaking starts
whats a safe place
whats a safe place

Bang that pan rig that sail

shake that megavoice

shake that microtone

wake the intergang ok ok

dont go back in hold the game

with our softness with our give

Here is matters vessel
ok the sum is sunsail
ok the sum of friends
ok the sum is earnt
ok the sum well worked

Let the light shake your bones

let the light shake your bones

let the light the ground the tides

shake yr bones

ok the ground started shaking

Here is ok
mind home embodies ok
walk inside your own walk
sit inside your own seat
talk within your own voice
spread within your own shape

Language started shaking
ok the day started shaking
ok words are a matter of shaking
ok openly handled
ok ok turn gold to goats

Your legs are the legs of legs

your arms are the arms of arms

your face is the face of face

let the tides

when the shaking starts

Let the tides shake your life
let your life shake the ground
until your bones are bonedust
until your smile is smiledust
until your courage is delivered
ok ok until it is done

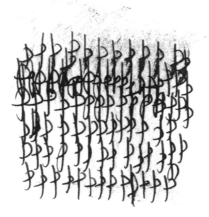

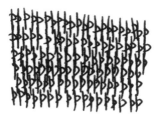

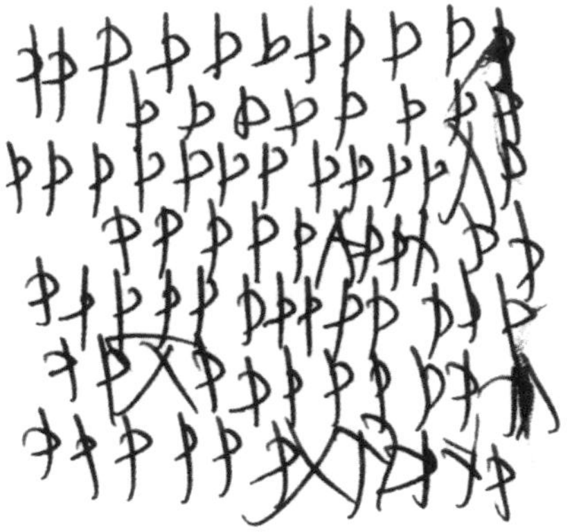

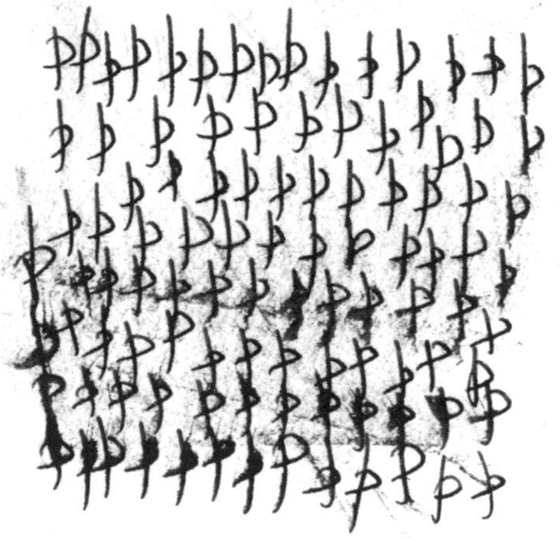

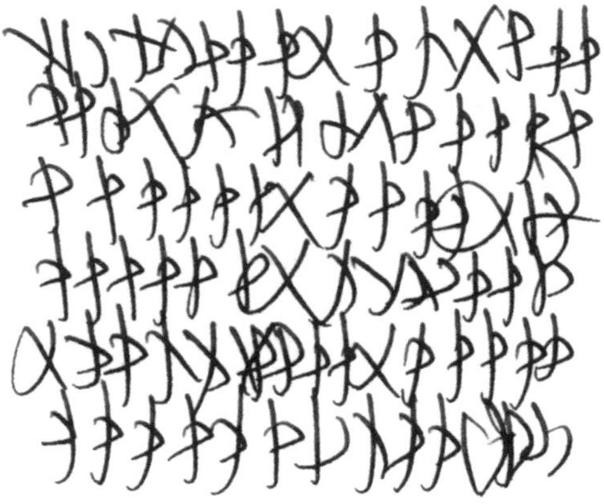

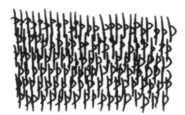

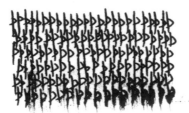

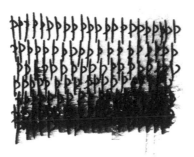

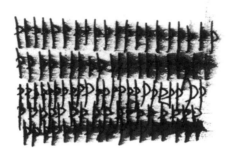

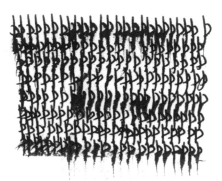

LOG

What is north. Is it a direction or a process. A method or a place. Is it space accelerated into time, like a glacial flood. Is it time spread into space, like permafrost. Is it always further on, further north until it makes a vertical drop, like a voice that traverses, illuminates everything but will not itself be held. Is it trajectory or endpoint, or both.

<u>Early medieval open sea navigation</u>
build a seaworthy ship
tar the ship in autumn
keep it tarred in winter
travel in summer
use strong oars
use steady gear
stay close to the coastline
check with a lead line
travel from landmark to landmark
use sails
check the prevailing wind

go by the stars

use polaris

go by the sun

check the currents

go by types of birds

go by the movements of fish and sea mammals

→The plan is to write a text for live voice, percussion and electronic text. To explore the archaic, tribal traffic between voice and drum, between text and beat, between air and skin, voice and breathing. The graphic and visual dimension of the text will deepen my exploration of installed textual work through a live setting. It all feels like a logical development of my work, this push to a more substantial and collaborative form of vocality, this more sustained and extended physicality and musicality of the performed text, this explicit turn towards the skaldic, shout-out traditions of poetic delivery. To go deep down in time and in body, to bare bones, to dust bones, while also very much rooted in the technological traffic and energy of performance. To be sounding language, to be calling it up to an audience. Calling up the messengers, root-words, stem-sounds, flowering lines that have nurtured and kept the voices that now have me and egg me on into

the story. I start work with the Norwegian percussionist Ingar Zach. His intense search for resonance and vibration taps into flows and thoughts inside me. One of the first pieces we try together is a version of Tim Buckley's "Song to the Siren" reduced to a pattern of ceramic bells and spoken song. I place my voice inside his sound and let it do its work. It's just practice and it feels great. At night in my hotel room I try to write but I'm too exhausted from the physical impact of spending hours inside these sounding and spoken vibrations. There's a constant electric buzz running through my limbs.

Long afloat on shipless oceans
I did all my best to smile
'Til your singing eyes and fingers
Drew me loving to your isle
And you sang
Sail to me
Sail to me
Let me enfold you
Here I am
Here I am
Waiting to hold you

The radical Grü/Transtheatre in Geneva invites me to create a performance for their closing festival. One of its directors, Michèle Pralong, becomes involved in the production of the work. Working together is precise and pleasurable. Other things start to shake me up. I decide to use the anonymous Anglo-Saxon poem "The Seafarer" as one of the central pieces of the performance and as a template to my own writing. I am deeply affected by this tenth-century medieval quest poem written by an anonymous poet-sailor. Reading it with a literal word-to-word translation, the Seafarer's stark, repetitive and sorrowful beating at the waves and at the soul resonates with me in more ways than one. Yet in its original language the text evades me nearly completely. I stumble on the largely incomprehensible quality of the Old English language, the obsolete letters, the pervasive syntactical declension, its internal poetic rhyming and chain of alliterations, the repetitive and compact narration, very little of which can be accessed via contemporary English. Indeed at times it feels easier to think of it in relation to historical Norwegian, another language I know next to nothing about.

Maeg ic be me sylfum

Make me / let me / have me

May I / can ic / can ache

Ache / ache / ic

ic – ache: the slip acceptable orally

ache to me myself and I

sodgied // sop – true real righteous // soppgiedd – true tale

siþ – nm going movement journey expedition / also as as some sort
of suffix?

April 12. In a first instance, I have decided to keep myself at a safe
distance from the old text: paraphrasing, creating narrative, veering
off into sound sense, not diving too much into the materiality of the
language itself. All the while having to recognise the increasingly
mysterious, unnerving pull of a vaster transformation taking place
inside my life and my work. So I let the writing find its place, work its
way, without asserting too much control.

<u>wrecan</u>

Let me speak my true journeys

ache wracked from travel

out there ne safety

ache sacrificed all parts of me

on battered shipu
suffered biting despair
gebruised by sea chops
endured dark burrows,
during many a nightwaco
bearing too close to the clifs
was bitterly tested
cursed with nightmares
collapsed into weird comas
inner waves clubber me
wishing, reeling, dawn hunger release me
Blow wind blow, anon am I

11 April 2012. An article in *The Guardian* outlines a report just published by *Forensic Oceanography* (Goldsmiths University) and developed by two researchers, Charles Heller and Lorenzo Pezzani: "Migrant boat tragedy: UK crew may have seen doomed vessel." The manner in which 72 migrants had been left to perish on their way from Tripoli to Lampedusa in full view of a number of patrolling vessels had caused shock and widespread outrage the previous year and had become known as the "Left-to-Die Boat case." In keeping

with the strongly interdisciplinary fieldwork methodologies as well as judicial underpinning of the new field of forensic architecture, the researchers have painstakingly pieced together the seemingly untraceable activities surrounding this tragic event. The report will now be used as part of an international court case set up by human rights' lawyers.

sodgied wrecan siþas secgan
sods' gate true tale telling
wrecan – to tell
wraec – exile
wrecan – misery
wraecca – stranger / exile / wretched
wraeclic – skrekkelig
wreccan – awake / arouse encourage
wacian – weaken / lose courage/ fall

Executive summary
In order to generate our analysis and report we employed a wide range of digital mapping and modelling technologies, which included the use of Synthetic Aperture Radar (SAR) imagery, geospatial mapping,

and drift modelling. In collecting, analysing, and synthesising data, reports, and human testimonies related to the case, this report reconstructs as accurately as possible what happened to this vessel.

geswincdagum /
dagum plural acc?
Norw. svine / to burn
Norw. svikte – let down –
Norw. forsvinne – disappear - disappear in the warp
screw up, wind up
smite, slap, thump, beat, lay on, twist (in the wind)

The forensic principle: that every action or contact leaves a trace. I decide to use the narrative of the journey and its harrowing drift, the story told by the survivors and corroborated by the forensic findings. My role will be to shorten the narrative and relay the report's complex piece of memorialisation, interpretation and investigation through live recitation. To register the event by recitation. Letting the recitation become a resonating chamber, a ripple effect. Insistent methods in art are intimately connected to processes of receiving and of following. One loads ones vessel for dream-travel and one follows it into hell. A

reciting voice remains simultaneously input and output. Resonance is contact ripple. Everything is connected in the vast chamber of the world, beyond the callous, brutal politics. Everything ripples at contact.

<u>dag – day dock deck</u>
to swingdangle on deck for days
ge- using the prefix, in OE mainly preterit forms of weak (?check) verbs
also as pret + adverbial?
check on use and / or simply for emphasis [or what attribute?] when using with some verbs?
gebang
gedangle
gebash
geget

15 June 2012. The success of the first performance, the connection between Ingar's playing and my work, the report read live in more or less complete darkness, the audience's intense response, my Norwegian father's inspiring presence at it, the disturbance that is pushing a way into my life, all this leaves me in a total state of shock

and openness. I come home and find that I have lost my sense of home.
I come home to find that I have left my home. No rest, no refuge.

earfoðhwile

prep? shifter

here for a while / all the while /

as noun:

earfoðhwile f hard time

earfoð / earfeðe full of hardship, troublesome, difficult

earfoþsìþ difficult journey, toilsome journey

eare – ark : chest box coffin, Noahs ark. Latin arca

corr to runic letter

ēar m sea

ēargrund – depths of the sea

ēarp earth

ear – eáre OE –

shared across germanic languages – ON eyra

Latin auris – Old Irish - ó

Earful - Sound in the ear / loudness of the wind / loud

in the err – northern pronunc - more recent term, 13thc – French

erre

To be reminded of the thick fogs in the Midlands when driving home at night. My car-lights would hit back at me like a mirror. Driving with no lights and at 10 mph for fear of driving off the road. After a few minutes the night would slowly open up. Driving home by turning the lights on and off whenever the road ahead and the absence of facing cars allowed.

bıtre breostceare gebıden hæbbe
at heart - care?
OED: OE breost ON *brjóst neutral plural*
"*Breust-* cannot be connected with *berstan, brestan* to burst: but it may be related to the Old Saxon vb. *brustian* to bud" + "Each of the two soft protuberances situated on the thorax in females"
fig. seat of affections, the heart, private, feelings: in pl. in OE breoste ?chck)

To separate, to leave someone, is to leave everything. Everything planned, known, secured, released, fine-tuned, structured, achieved is now upended in a way that exceeds comprehension. The solid structure is collapsing in on itself. What is a solid structure. The hard boundary that one crashes into. The course I hold is stubborn and at

times necessarily myopic. I shut out my eyes, my ears, all my senses to what I have set in motion. I can only trust what is taking place, but how to trust fear, and how to trust pain.

<u>OE kare n / k- air /</u>
OE caru cearu — here w case?
Suffering / mental, sorrow, grief
cœur? Centre?
ON kör / gen karar: bed of trouble or sickness
Also vb cearian — here vb? To sorrow to grieve
No combined noun , verb next clause:
breast care: breast suffering: heartgrief, core suffering / grief

I take the whole performance apart. I discard the work done, the open feeling experienced on the night. I am left with nothing but a chaotic gaping construction site. Why.

<u>gebiden hæbbe</u>
have / had
bidan? Tr. Endure, experience —
also pray se Norw å be

had endured /
heart bidding
habits
the bidding of pain

Total fumbling. The fog in my mind, my life, my heart. Perhaps it is great on paper to find oneself after a long period of loss. In reality of course, it's just dark and dirty. Being lost while holding on is simply getting stuck. Being stuck is the most lost. I return to the old sailor but it still keeps me in check. Being lost is a way of inhabiting space by registering what is not familiar, writes Sara Ahmed. Like coming out of orbit, going into freefall, MAYDAY MAYDAY MAYDAY, registering blinding panic or unexpected calm, depending on one's preparedness or willingness to fall. In that same book, she uses the phrase sexual orientation in a literal sense, like a compass in a terrain, to spatialise sexuality into directional dynamics: "It matters how we arrive at the place we do". I find it helpful, nearly comforting to think that my current unfocused trajectory, its temporary dwelling spaces and my previously mapped-out travelling could be seen as so many illuminated dots of the way. As though each uprooting, each departure, each arrival does create deep magnetic oscillations across

the entire spectrum of travelling and dwelling. The growing reality of collective departures and arrivals would need to be experienced as dynamic pattern formations, generative in a programming sense of the way they affect any port of call. The textual dimension of the performance will a few months later be composed with the artist and programmer Thomas Köppel as a projected language-mass, the visual accumulation of the entire finished textual material. All of it laid out, then overlaid, set in motion and activated through a generative pattern of sequences. The sequences turn the text into a deep-moving, slow-changing multi-dimensional hypnotic wave. A vast open syntax of textual mass. The elements move around one another, are drawn and repelled, answer to separate yet co-extensive syntactical instances. It will take me a long time to understand how to do it and how to get there.

Navigation instruction
stay calm

Passing out many times years ago during a period of excessive exhaustion from work and partying and substances. Coming home, putting the key through the door, walking in only to wake up, seconds or minutes later flat out on the floor and bruised from the fall. I would crawl into bed.

Nights would teem with nightmares from my overheating body. No recollection ever of these recurrent falls. No memory.

cunnan ? – kjenne / bekjent? cnow
cēol – ship // ceole – throat // Fr. ciel
cear / selda – see above
cearseld n place of sorrow
cursed
cear?

gecunnad in ceole cearselda fela atol yÞa gewealc
(work at a shadowing)

The previous year we had redone our flat in order to get rid of the dampness seeping through the ground floor. The builder dug the whole floor out. The more he was digging the more layers of dampness and rot and decomposed matter he was uncovering. I was hoping he would uncover a small burial ground, or at the very least a small fossil. The hole deepened. Full of dark, wet and rotting wood and soil and decomposed bricks. In the end he was nearly two meters down and more than two skips with filthy stinking waste stuff had

been filled and carried off. The hole was deeper than a hole. The hole seeped through everything. It invaded the whole flat and our minds. Filled us up with holeness. What is a hole. What does one do when a hole takes over space it has not been allocated. When it starts to behave like not a hole, a not hole, a solid block of not-matter matter.

Navigation instruction

prepare

tighten

release

wait

•

July 12. I have been awarded a Fellowship in Cambridge on the basis of this rewrite. The Fellowship is housed within their thriving English and Anglo-Saxon Studies department. I move into the Fellows' quarters. This brings respite from the inner and outer chaos. I spend weeks plundering books and facsimiles taken down from the open shelves. I lose myself avidly in the cold corridors, in the busy silence, in the book-lined labyrinthine miles.

<u>Þær mec oft bigeat nearo nihtwaco</u>
there / where meg often - get?
use: during many a nightwaco
nearo is not near or nær – but narrow, confined, limited
accompanied by distress
there I often got
å bære seg – burden

Nov 12. Four months of intense research and I feel totally stumped.
This is not a translation project yet it feels as though I'm working it
that way. I suppose it is what I have to go on. How can I free myself
from the original text without relinquishing the historical language
altogether since this does remain the red thread of the entire project.
How can I find an archaeological or forensic method that will help
me generate a way of writing that can both speak to today and safely
point to tagged and numbered teeth items in the ground. How can I
find the tools necessary to dig at whatever is driving me.

<u>fela adv much</u>
fell / felled / fellow
yfel (awful) adj. decl. bad painful miserable

atol adj. terrible dire horrid

I work some of it out by sound association. By engaging with the source text in a loose homophonic call and response, I can both cut away from the less yielding aspects of this transhistoric contact and value the strongly sound-led rules of the original. Nominative compounds, weird suffixes, chains of phonemic repetitions also help create syntactical and rhythmical inroads. I pretend to a possible one-to-one sound-to-sound assimilations, indulge in false friends and fake slippages, flatten out etymologies and historic developments. In this manner, I make some progress.

gewealc n. rolling sea, struggle, battle
+ rolling / wringing ? – also of body stomach, sickness – wringing
in OE of a cider press
beknown / have known
in this ship of sorg / trouble / troubled ship
cursed in ship of sorg gewacked by sea chops

Every morning I go to work. It is a constant return to blankness. Like some sort of amnesia or lesion, I can't recognise or understand the

work done the previous day. It is the strangest feeling this impossibility to make and retain sense. I can't organise things into a reassuring distance nor a semblance of a functioning structure. Most of the time, I feel nauseous, lethargic, disorientated. The state of my unravelling condition during this whole period is perhaps best described by the following event. One afternoon my friend Rod Mengham takes me to the small Fellows' Garden in Jesus College. A plaque by the artist Cornelia Parker commemorates the moon landing: "On the night of the full moon, 22 June 2005, a piece of the moon fell in this garden. It wasn't a natural phenomenon but a deliberate homeopathic act; a fragment of a lunar meteorite was allowed to fall from my hand and to disappear in the terrain. It had fallen once before, after eons circulating in space it was eventually captured by earth's gravitational pull, landing in North Africa, part of a chain of events that have led to this garden." Needless to say, the meteorite has long since again orbited away from the garden. The whole piece was so accurately absurd, so meanderingly, lovingly shruggable that my immediate kneejerk reaction was quickly followed by the most blissful sense of relief. So many meteorites, so many hands, so many terrains, so many leads, so many ways to see land.

Navigation instruction

accept

that you are being pushed about

work small, close-up

No longer expecting to make it to the other side, or any other side,
I open up the process to the accidents of the gravitational pull. I
check my pockets for space fossils, meteoritic gravel. I stop writing
in order to prepare for it. I become fascinated by the medieval ruling
lines with which scribes would prepare the parchment for writing
and for illustration, and the various tools they developed for greater
regularity and to speed up the tedious preparations. Line follows
line follows lines. Horizontals, verticals. There are squares left for
the opening illumination. Initially the idea is to have them be pretty
regular and neatly spaced-out as though they would be encasing a
text. After hours and days enjoying this slightly spaced-out, aimless
and compensatory activity, gestures have become comfortable and
have started to integrate the pace. But now the lines are starting to
think of their own accord. They refuse the ruler, refuse their line
state, thicken and deepen and engage in short dances that release
other spatial rhythms. They start to behave like the faint trackings

of sounds or movements, imaging sonars or spectographs, in their capacity to adjust and respond to my movements and drops in attention. It is as though the lines were on the lookout for something. The medieval quest poem sought its purpose and spiritual nature in the testing, frightening yet also inspiring symbiosis of the geographic and the symbolic journey. Its many accidental encounters and obstacles were made readable by the quest itself. Often written as a mix of mythical, poetic and actual journeys, these texts have also helped chart the geographical contours of the North Atlantic's many coasts and islands. Joining the dots, writing up the oscillations and the coastlines any way we can.

Medieval North Atlantic journeys & sites
the Vinland sagas
the Greenlanders sagas
Gudrid Gudridur's voyages
Eirik the Red's saga
the Poetic Edda
The Voyage of Bran
the Voyage of St Cuthbert
Arab geographers and the Sea of Perpetual Gloom

the Voyage of St Brendan

Orosius' Thule

the Voyage of Ohthere of Hågaland

the Journey of Wulfstan of Hedeby

King Alfred's North

Knud Rasmussen's *Fifth Thule Expedition*

Glenn Gould's *The Idea of North*

Ewan Mccoll's radio ballad *Singing The Fishing*

Ingeborg Bachmann's *Songs From An Island*

Thomas Köner's treated field recordings *Nunatak, Teimo, Permafrost*

Anya Gallacio's melting ice sculpture *Intensities and Surfaces*

These days travelling great distances by sea is mainly done for luxurious leisure, or as a last resort. It is the last option. How many overfilled open boats fleeing war zones and political oppression have resorted to dangerous, clandestine crossings of the Mediterranean Sea, of the Sicily Channel, of the Aegean sea, of the Caribbean sea, of the Red Sea, of the Gulf of Thailand, of the South China Sea. I remember the arrival of the Vietnamese boat people in Norway in the 1970s. They were the first larger collective wave of refugees immigrating to this northern, underpopulated and proudly insular country.

Calde geÞrungen wæron mine fet

forste gebunden caldum clommum

Not sure how phonically or how tight to go here

Kulle? Kulla? Seems to bring in ON character!

The cold clasp of kulla

Keeps opening it up to northern direction

Opacity as some sort of compositional as much as existential reality
yields tough lessons about knowledge and applying one's skills.
Tough lessons about investigation. Tough lessons about not looking
too soon for the surf and the break. Being lost had shut down the field
of thinking, of sensing, and choosing one's tracks. It left no choice.
No illumination nor guiding light, just to draw lines and insist and
push on through the sea-sickness and the confusing solitude of desire.
This is another kind of separation. It arises not from the past but from
what's to come, not from the familiar but from the unimagined, the
potential arrival. Desire's opacity is the longing that gives the courage
to depart, to set out. It lends the harshest sweetness to the most
total risk. It is as opaque as it is luminous and precious. The desired
intensity of its luminosity always much depends on the political
times one lives in and how much darkness is imposed as light.

To measure the light in order to make out other objects in the night. How much freedom can be retained and explored from dwelling in the dark, how much work can be released when making it out into the light. How much release when making out the nature of darkness and light, and walking into it.

mod —mind intellect, heart, pride
/ Norw. mot? courage/
merewerges – whats this? / mera nightmare? / merewerig sea weary
/ mereweard sea guardian
slat – sliter

No longer do I know how to get from A to Z now that I have to deal with Þ and æ and ð and œ and gendering and declension all over the place. Always gender and declension and kinship. Always language acquisition will harbour new modes of arrival and arrivants. But trying now to walk away from this original template-text would be like cutting myself off from all language. I know only what is here. All languages and all my languages now flow from it. And how could I renounce the desire I feel for her when it is so mysteriously tied to a logic that is so much bigger than my own.

heortan – heart hjerte /

hungor innan - Keep hungor innan as good Norw. connection here
hunger within
within without

Passing out many times years ago at the club from drugs and
dehydration, I'm shook up, woken up by the paramedic saying,
What's your name, What's your name. I look at him. He has the most
beautiful face. Intense rays of light emanate from his jacket. Are you
St Christopher. Are you Our Lady of Safe Travel. This is the rescue,
am I safe.

foldan – earth/ground/surface – land
OE folde
ON fold
surface of the earth, the ground
the fold, leave, fold,
fold out across the iscaldne weg way

To remind myself that this project is not an exercise in translation,
however closely I work with the original text. It is a template for

writing. And for excavating language. For finding the teeth of my own text, for locating its workable memory trails. Bizarrely it has also become a template for tackling the painful obtuse persistence of the unfolding events in my life. I remind myself that this text was made for speaking. It will again be spoken, it will again resonate, exhale, be sung. It will again dissipate in the vibratory rhythms of the percussion, it will again disperse in the skull, in the live space, in the responsive skin of the audience. To this end, it must flow, it must position itself in relation to the air and the winds. Its seaworthiness as it were must be found not only through the knots and bolts and ropes and lines and planks and hull structure of its linguistic research, but also in its capacity to catch the wind itself and to sail with it. It must be on the look-out for the wind and the currents and the flow of the travel as much as it insists on building a functioning c/raft.

seofedun vb fed up
seo – if use as vision rather than sea
/ doesn't work here yet blind for seeing
seon vb seofian vb lament

The drifting gathers pace. I turn to my Nordic heritage. Its deep

connection with the cold and the dark seas doubles up on the Anglo-Saxon islander's own coastal and seabound reality. The sagas are written in a descriptive repetitive prose, most likely from oral accounts. Being both travel and settlement stories, many describe episodes of being lost at sea. They call it hafville, sea wilderness, sea wildering. Initially I simply quote from translations of a few of the Icelandic sagas. Slowly I then let them spin the work deeper towards the heart of the fog.

FOG n. 1
dict of etymo online: "thick, obscuring mist," 1540s, probably from a Scandinavian source akin to Dan. fog "spray, shower, snowdrift," O.N. fok "snow flurry," fjuk "snow storm." Cf. also O.E. fuht, Du. vocht, Ger. Feucht "moist."

This new section brings up a tense, performative rhythm to the work. Sailing starts to take place in the unfolding of the graphic work, in the textual scape, in the spatial markers. Writing becomes tracks and traces and lines. Patiently it stays afloat and waits for a time, draws a way back towards language. It emerges from tracking, and from throwing up on deck what had seemingly disappeared from both the

past and the future.

FOG. n 2.

dict of etymo online: "long grass," c.1300, probably of Scandinavian origin, cf. Norwegian fogg "long grass in a moist hollow," Icelandic fuki "rotten sea grass." The connection to fog (n.1), via a notion of long grass growing in moist dells of northern Europe, is tempting but not proven. Watkins suggests derivation from PIE *pu- "to rot, decay."

Eventually one comes to a point where being lost can signal a starting-point and can become its own type of activity. Needing guides, I return to Cixous and Glissant. I look to Sukhdev Sandhu's *Nighthaunts*, Yoko Tawada's *Journal des Jours Tremblants*, David Toop's *Haunted Weather*. Their drifting brings up intimate knowledge of disappearances, oscillations, soundwaves, apparitions. Or Pasolini's fireflies lighting up a political and sexual-cultural way in the Italian night. Or Edwin Morgan translating his *Beowulf* on returning traumatised from WW2. Just as I'm closing this work some six months later, Ana Mendieta's retrospective at the Hayward Gallery retraces the ritualised bodily connection between prehistoric shapes and her haunting live burials, materialised in her *silhuetas*. To reorient oneself. To go east. To get l

ost.

se mon ne wat
the man not knows
Þæt se mon ne wat
Þe him on foldan
fægrost limpeð
hu ic earmcearig iscealdne sæ
winter wunade wræccan lastum,
winemægum bidroren,
bihongen hrimgicelum; hægl scurum fleag.
fiær ic ne gehyrde butan hlimman sæ, iscaldne wæg.

Glissant keeps medieval literature and its nomadic sociality always present and at work in his own wanderings. I turn to ancient initiatory journeys, on sea or on land, travellers on a mission. Some strip to the bone. Some count the days. Some sing of strange sights and terrors. All lose themselves. All give up. All lose some life to it. All persist. I go back to Eliane Radigue's *Songs of Milarepa*, Robert Ashley's sleep-awake voice in the right channel, the Tibetan lama Lama Kunga's voice in the left channel. To reorient oneself. To go east. To go lost. To go naught.

To north oneself. To come to song. What does it mean in practical terms. Magnifying the process. Working at a standstill. Opening up to a drastic vertical drop. Being tilted vertically, Hiroshi Sugimoto's *Revolution*, dark silvery moonscapes, turn the flat horizon line into a 90 degree precipitation of gravity. The viewing process becomes compressed with vertical energy and a mysterious serenity.

mon
– one in the sense of someone?
manna/monn/mann – human being
Mon – shortened name for the Monoceros constellation
fægrost – rost Norw. røst stemme: voice
// Norw. fager: beautiful
earmcærig – Norw. øm kjaer - dear

The OED mentions the origin of "fog" as uncertain. Points to the long grass and does not mention the weather system. Fog memory loss identity loss. SIGNAL LOSS. Damaged documents. Fog out the voice the words. Formally as much as existentially. Phenomenologically and perceptually: create a landscape of signals. By constantly changing perspectives and viewing distances, Wolfgang Tillmans' *Truth Study*

Centre speeds up the disparate aspect of the work, yet slows down its cumulative photographic knowledge. Slows down, slows down, slows down one's absorption of the images. Slows down the viewing process. I work with the photographer Tom Martin at macro magnification. I want to use the surveillance photo of the migrants taken by the French military aircraft at the start of their journey in the zodiac. I need to make sure that we can work through but not cancel out the uneasy sick feeling I get when peering down from the future at this image. Tom has photographed people and faces for NGOs in many difficult conflict zones and has a quiet demeanour about the importance of portraiture. But we are working here with a pre-existing image. It encounters the dead as they are still living and sailing. The macro processing of the image is a process of collapsed timespace, of enhanced slowing down, of active registering. It lifts the inscription of their sailing pixel by pixel from the fog of incessant newsrush and quick apparitions and swift forgetting. It insists on being seen and rescued. The macro work investigates the traces of other ghosts. One notices rows of yellow dots on the surface of the macro print that hide all sorts of locational information about the printer and printing process.

Navigation instruction
work large, as in sailing large
utilise all skills and craft
look for the wind

To fall in love against all odds is to leave everything behind. Everything planned, known, secured, released, fine-tuned, structured, achieved is now upended in a way that exceeds comprehension. Everything shuts down to open to something else. Against all odds to be swept out, far out, to be dared and challenged at core. It is a form of wisdom-madness the intense absolute way in which this love calls.

Navigation instructions
make sure it can be spoken
make sure it will be spoken

ForÞon: Because/ Therefore/ Indeed
for some / indeed / in this way /
ForÞon nis Þæs /
Modwlonc: Norw. mot / courage
Wlonc: wlanc: proud – elated – grand / Norw. stolt

Because not there is. Not yet migrants and skraelings not yet.

Use the 8 fordon structurally

Crossing/ knust / now / broken now nu

Thats why thats why thats why thats why thats why thats why thats

why thats why

Heart geographies/ thoughts/

Heart gethinking/ full of thoughts

That ache for the high/ hard streams

The Salt tysse/ tossing tyÞa tireless seas/streams /waves

Self I know/ cunnige: strive / should strive / conch/

monad modes lust / monthly mood wishes / more mood wishes

lust – desire/ lyst

salt of the mind – mind salt

I apply myself to transforming desire into a sense of pleasure. To feel
everything without the need for possession. It's a way of surviving
the irreducible shock. And of accepting an impossible turning back.
Staying afloat using all I have to hand without jumping in too quickly
and without losing all elements on the way. Keeping heart and
making slow ingress. Leave the mould to enter this trajectory. This is
the rescue, are we safe.

Medieval novigation

no engines

no fuel

no magnetic compasses

no sea charts

no logs

no global positioning systems

no C-maps

no Automatic Radar Plotting Aids

no echo sounding systems

no digital depth sounders

no National Oceanic and Atmospheric Association broadcasts

no Global Maritime Distress and Safety System

no satellite phone

no shipping forecasts

no inmarsat systems

no SAR Search And Rescue responsibility zone for coastal states

no 1982 United Nations Convention on the Law of the Sea

no 1974 International Convention for the Safety of Life at Sea

no NATO Naval and Aerial monitoring

no coffee

no cocoa

Glissant, Brathwaite. They chart another historic Atlantic, further south. The horrors of the Middle Passage, the genocidal crossing which robs of all identity, the enslaved survivors' arrival, which robs the arrivants of whatever's left of: name, language, history, family, song, body, health, freedom. The making of their poetics declares the impossibility of return and the laying down of roots. Once crossed always crossed. Yet their insights reject the tabula rasa of a history of conquerors and obliterators. Languages work in profound ways. They intermingle and act as obscure relays of one another. They call up all the languages of the world

ferd to feran
repeat from my first version
add
frefran = freefrom = free form

For all one can say about love's deep process of reconnection with forgotten impulses and discarded knowledges, at first it really provides no grounding, no view, no balance, no safety, no future. Bare bones. Much cruelty to this beauty. It eradicates any certainty one could have had about one's own trajectory and general motivations. And any

thoughts one could have had about one's ability to remain impervious to disabling change. Remorselessly it seduces with horizonless plane after horizonless plane. Relentlessly it rips the heart out of all rest and any refuge. Chaos and illumination. To prevent the full impact of this vertigo, I hole up with my work. Bizarre mythological wordbeasts and flying creatures move in with me.

Because gelifts little /
Therefore gelifted a bit
See the / them ah at life's wine / winnings
Who Gelive in the city
bealosifla hwon
wlonc ok wino
how ache weary often
sceolde : endure/ scolded/

Other beings board the workshop. The first giants. The ones called jötnar, Þursar, mountain risers. They bring out their wondrous spectacle. Their many heads, their enormous bodies, their procreating armpits and toes, their flaming tongues spitting out "thurs," dark magic nonsense. Some emerge from the rocks, others from

underwater earthquakes. From their flesh, the earth was formed. From their bones, the rocks. The sky escaped from the skull of the ice-cold giant Ymir. The sea, from his blood.

Tidege:
one's time/ one's tide/one's timing – "final day"
OÞÞe
OÞÞe
"up you get up you get" Jarman's *The Garden*
tear / torn from this world

I remain very confused about what to do with the narrative and poetic break in the second half of the text. It moves the high lyricism and textual beauty about the sea and exile and renunciation into a poetically less developed and strongly didactic Christian moral tale. There are longstanding controversies about this break and many maintain that is likely two writers have written this text at two different periods, the circumatsances of which remain totally unknown. If nothing else, there is definitely a during and an after. Some of the early Christian precepts on impermanence, living the life of the death you want, praising the glorious dead present in this

second half remind me of the gnomic sayings in the Poetic Edda. Also the Buddhist boddhisattvas, and the lives of saints.

70
feorh oðpringeð
72
And now
æftercweÞendra / ettervandring / after death / [of those who speak afterwards]
lof lifgendra

Also Tibetan and Zen spiritual travels. Transformative renunciations. Milarepa naked in the mountain storm holding on for dear life by one last branch. Transformative release. The storms walked me down to her shore. The storms took me to her sea. Illumination comes in the shape of the love I feel for her. It comes in the shape of our true love's courage. Love as the motivation and driver of art. Love as the transformative driver of more life. Art as a process of shared life. As a process of love acquisition. Genealogies of love and lovers. Voices that rise from the drop, that come through the fog of my skin.

lastworda betst
that he geworks
is on bis way scyle
forward on earth
dearum dædum
dearoh dear

There is much at stake. Chaos and illumination. Each we must break
up camp. Each we must be both lost and found. To be with her I
must undo what I know. To be with me, she must tell her husband,
her kids, her family. A deep animal fear at this profound and life-
changing impulse also resurfaces in me. Are you safe. One's known
sense of protection and more or less highly developed self-defense
mechanisms give the bounds and the coastlines and ultimately the
horizon to one's being. To be protected in law gives a further collective
implication to it. Families, vigilantes and coastguards can no longer
in all impunity go to work on those it has taken to be halflings and
skraelings. But the menacing fear and the deep collective memory
remain at the point of crossing, at the point of sailing, as one
raises the anchor, as one ships out. They are sustained in the more
obscure aspects of one's living and re-engage in full force in the

face of others who still must live in abject lawlessness, in different degrees of hideout. Are you safe. I want the project to end, to reach its voiced and resounding completion, to start a new journey under its sounding protection. A profound joy starts to cut the strings that have held me to my fears. I need to join her, I need to rejoin friends and communities, have a decent hot meal, engage in open work. Let me come in from the cold cold way, Seafarer.

hyht: joy? Hope? [see diff translations]
Þonc
Punk/ thump
= thanks (be)/

NOÞING

Its a fine day • you step on to the top soil of your strata • you trip over some þing nearly makes you fall over • you look down but cant see any þing • for a few days this continues • youre walking along • enjoying the air the light the traffic the vast city around you • whatever • your foot trips on some þing • you catch yourself look down but no theres no þing there • a few days later • its a fine day youre walking • in a pensive mood a lively mood a stressed out mood a sad mood • no matter • your foot gets caught on some þing • makes you trip not not fall • catch yourself • look down or back cant see anyþing at all •

Later that week its a fine day • your foot gets caught • you trip not not fall catch yourself • look down • back slightly • tarmac smooth and clear • no þing there at all • get caught trip not not fall catch yourself look down no þing • get caught trip not not fall catch yourself look back no þing • caught trip not not fall • catch yourself no þing • get caught trip catch yourself • þing • caught trip c tch your lf • þing • caught trip n t fall tch þing • c tch þing • þing • c tch its a fine day walking along foot gets caught • trip c tch yourself • þing • c tch •

þing for a few ticks all is caught quiet c þing in suspension • in a perfect tripping suspension •

This is totally flipping • you look down • its a fine day • caught in quiet susp • theres a small root or a stone sticking up from the tarmac • just under your foot • keeping you perfectly susp • ended • a very small root or a stone is upsticking from the strata top layer tarmac • you bend down to pull at it • it isnt a root at all nor is it a stone • looks more like a bone or a tooth • could be a large wooden oar with carvings from an old sunken ship • looks very much like a tooth • clean it up with your sleeve • def no þing like any tooth youve ever seen • not like the tooth you had removed the other day • its more like a • or some þing •

You put the tooth in your mouth • doesnt fit at all now thats a relief • feels like a large sail in your mouth • its big it pulls at your jaw • you put it in your mouth you feel a great pull a great cold of some þing • a great blan of dust a taste of ash þings your mouth covers your teeth your tongue • dust rushes out fills your mouth þing • need air • not need air • a great ash cloud starts to spin • spinning ash fills the vocal cavities • a sound like a sound that is mine yet not mine starts to spin

in the mouth • sounds spin in the hole of the mouth • sounds ring
to the hole like voices ringing in the hole of the muð of my mouth •
mouth þing much like mine yet not mine •

Its a fine day • dust crowds pay my mouth a visit • dust voices like
mine yet not mine • ringing in the hol • dust voices ash clouds in my
mouth on this fine day • ðes fine day ðes fine dæg • ash clouds of the
dead the dust bein of the daudr on ðes fin dæg • ðes fine day • the
dúst bàn of the daudr • fine day fin dæg • fill my mouth up • ring in
min muð on ðes fin dæg • they fill min mund on ðes fin dæg • they
fill min up • fill me up on ðes fin dæg • open my muð for the þing of
the hol • the þing of my mouþ for the sound of the hol • listen here
hear the sound on ðes dæg • ring on ðes day • nu listen nu here hear
ring on ðes fin dæg • denne fine dæg •

þ

I went looking for my Nordic roots in the English language and found this sign. A p attached to a long stick, or a type of hoop. Apparently, my Norwegian folks were island pastors and seamen from the south-eastern part of the country. Would they have used such a tool? Perhaps as a walking stick or as a cleat for tying the rope once they had docked their boat. But not as a written sign. At any rate, I only know about my ascendants until the early 19th century, by which time this runic sign, the thorn sign, would have fallen into disuse in both the Norwegian and the English writing systems. It would already be found mainly on the red-painted slabs of raised runestones that littered both the surfaces and the geological depths of Swedish and Norwegian landscapes:

Here shall these stones stand, reddened with runes.

One such runestone was uncovered in a Swedish car-park as recently as April 2009. The news made the rounds of Scandinavian online papers:

"The runestone first surfaced in the autumn when church authorities in Vallentuna excavated an area around the church in order to lay new cables. But the historical artefact's runic inscriptions were covered in mud and earth and the rare find went unnoticed for several months."

At the time of writing this, September 2012, newsrooms here in England have gone wild over a crooked skeleton with a large gash in its skull, which is being unearthed at a large archaeological dig beneath a car park in the city of Leicester. Although there are still some doubts, it is thought that this may be the deformed remains of the reviled medieval king Richard the Third.

"We've taken teeth out under clean conditions from which we'll try and get DNA" says a member of the archaeological team to *The Guardian*.

If the teeth, along with the jaws, provide the framework for the most complex speaking sounds, it is one of their other remarkable features that they are the hardest material in the human body and can be preserved even when bones have long turned to dust. In terms of archaeological forensics, their enamel and calcified tartar deposits

provide a treasure of information for ancient human identification. In 2005, after many years of research, John Ashdown-Hill, a historian and genealogist, had telephoned one Joy Ibsen to inform her that her DNA results made her in all likelihood the 16th generation niece of the dreaded king and the only carrier of his DNA. As she has now died, it is her son, Michael Ibsen, a furniture-maker, who has been invited to be present at the carpark dig:

"I really hope it's him" says he.

As the DNA being tested is passed through the female line, indeed it really is a bummer for sociopathic crazos and psychopaths of the world that Michael's sister, who has no children, is the only one capable of passing this one on to the test-tube. Way to go, sister.

The period that concerns me stretches from the 7th to the 10th centuries, a pre-Conquest period when the thorn sign is already one of the only two left of the runic alphabet to have been kept within the Anglo-Saxon alphabet. For centuries, it had remained a known and useful figure in Anglo-Saxon manuscript culture before landing itself in the political upheavals and technological revolution of early

print culture. The mechanical vicissitudes of the thornless German letterpress used by Caxton and others had in effect finally put a stop to it. As no specific letter was cast, it is the digraph ‹th› that came to replace the thorn in written English from the beginning of the 15th century. This also removed one subtle sound correspondence from the written English. Writing would no longer mark a difference between a voiceless þeck ‹thick› and a voiced fæðmian ‹to fathom›, as it would have done with some interchangability in Old English.

The success and ultimate demise of the letter reflect the contingencies and accidents of writing. It is a mysterious and tantalising marker of the completely buried inscriptive and syntactical realities at the root of the English that we live within. It functions as an indice, a compressed reminder of the slow and radical overhaul towards greater simplification, mechanisation and spelling chaos to which the language in both spoken and written modes would be submitted. As a sign, the thorn becomes a fossil, a thick hook at the heart of British and Irish archeo-graphic culture.

As a sound it survives as one of the most specific and difficult ones

of the language. It is a voiceless stop sound, an unvoiced fricative, also called interdental fricative because it is produced with the tongue simultaneously pressing between the upper and lower front teeth. The tongue pushes between the teeth to emit a breathlike whistling, an unvoiced friction of air. This stop sound is quite a muscular event. It demands a highly controlled placing of the tongue before applying and interrupting a sudden and strong push of outbreath. Famously, the sound itself is one of the tings which makes English so difficult to get right. This local difficulty might well account for the historically fascinating state of the English dental apparatus. At any rate, it is no small wonder that this "theta" sound finds substitutes such as the short voiceless sibilant /s/ or the voiceless alveolar stop /t/ not only in its language variants but especially among late learners of the language, for whom it remains a vexing and more or less chronic obstruction.

SOURCES

Seafarer
Pages 25-57 — Textual work organised in three sections: "16 Songs," "North" and "Hafville." It uses and spins off from a great number of sources, including the medieval Anglo-Saxon poem *The Seafarer* and the Icelandic *Vinland Sagas*. Details of sources and research can be found in the "Log," pp. 125-165.

Sighting
Page 59 — Aircraft sighting photograph, *Report on the "Left-To-Die Boat"* (p.50). The caption reads: "On 27 March at 14:55 GMT, a French aircraft informed Rome MRCC of the sighting of a boat with about fifty persons on-board. The aircraft established the position of the boat and took a picture of the vessel that was sent to Rome MCRR."
Pages 60-65 and Cover image — Three macro treatments from the aircraft image of the zodiac vessel with passengers.
Image work composed by Tom Martin.

Report
Pages 69-79 — The text quoted is from the reconstitution narrative of the drift based on an interview with Daniel Haile Gebre and the research in "Report on the 'Left-To-Die Boat'" prepared by Forensic Oceanography (Charles Heller, Lorenzo Pezzani and Situ Studio), part of the European Research Council project Forensic Architecture, Centre for Research Architecture, Goldsmiths, University of London.

Maps
p. 81 — Drift model from the *Report on the "Left-To-Die Boat,"* p. 50
p. 82-83 — Ohthere's First Voyage
p. 84 — The Northern Line (London Underground)
p. 86 — London-Geneva
p. 87-88 — Zodiac
p. 89-90 — Great Wave off Kanagawa
Maps designed by Pablo Lavalley.

<u>Shake</u>
Includes very loose translations from the *Håvamål*, Gnomic poem of Norwegian origin to be found in the *Elder Poetic Edda*, one of the most celebrated anonymous early Norse literary manuscripts. Annotated edition and glossary used: *Håvamål*, ed. by David A.H. Evans (Viking Society for Northern Research, vol. 7, UCL, 2000).

<u>Noþing</u> and <u>Þ</u>
Commissioned by Lucy Ives at *Triple Canopy* (NY) online magazine as an audio-visual essay for their *Corrected Slogans* issue #17, Nov '12. Produced in partnership with the Museum of Contemporary Art Denver, as part of the exhibition *Postscript: Writing after Conceptual Art*, curated by Nora Burnett Abrams and Andrea Andersson.

CREDITS

All the material for this book was researched, created, written, drawn, composed and first performed between March 2012 and Dec 2013. Touring started May 2014. Many people and situations helped shape the project's various forms.

The Performance

Première —
Grü/Transtheatre, Geneva,
15 June 2012 (1st version)

Shorelines Literature Festival of the Sea,
Southend-on-Sea, 8 Nov 2013 (final version). Curated by Rachel Lichtenstein and Metal

Concept & Voice —
Caroline Bergvall

Sound composition & Percussion —
Ingar Zach

Electronic text —
Thomas Köppel

Dramaturgy —
Michèle Pralong

UK Touring production —
Penned in the Margins
Sound and Music

Voice coach —
Marj McDaid

Known supporters —
Arvid Bergvall, Aliette Bergvall, the Passengers on the London-Southend Coach, all Fellow Travellers

Into Memory Stacy Doris, Monica Ross sorely missed

The Book

Research Award —
The Judith E. Wilson Poetry & Drama Fellowship, University of Cambridge, July' 12 – June '13. Many thanks to Rod Mengham and Drew Milne.

First Publications —
"Seafarer" (first sections) in *Den Engelske Kanal 2013*, ed. by Jørn Svaeren (Kolon Forlag, Olso, 2013).
"Noþing" and "Þ" in *Triple Canopy #17* (Nov '12). Thanks to Lucy Ives.
"Hafville" in *Poetry* magazine (May '14). Thanks to Fred Sasaki.

Reference —
Charles Heller, Lorenzo Pezzani and Situ Studio, *Forensic Oceanography: Report on the Left-to-Die boat*, Goldsmiths, University of London, April '12.

Photographer —
Tom Martin

Readers —
Michèle Pralong, Erin Mouré, Susan Rudy

Graphic designer —
Pablo Lavalley

Publisher —
Stephen Motika

My warmest thanks to each of you

CONTENTS

Nightboat Books

Nightboat Books, a nonprofit organization, seeks to develop audiences for writers whose work resists convention and transcends boundaries. We publish book rich with poignancy, intelligence, and risk. Please visit our website, nightboat.org, to learn about our titles and how you can support our future publications.

The following individuals have supported the publication of this book. We thank them for their generosity and commitment to the mission of Nightboat Books:

Elizabeth Motika
Benjamin Taylor

In addition, this book has been made possible, in part, by a grant from the New York State Council on the Arts Literature Program.

State of the Arts

NYSCA